BERG

for Andy

BERG
Hilary Menos

seren

Seren is the book imprint of
Poetry Wales Press Ltd.
57 Nolton Street, Bridgend, Wales, CF31 3AE
www.seren-books.com

The right of Hilary Menos to be identified as
the author of this work has been asserted in accordance
with the Copyright, Designs and Patents Act, 1988.

ISBN: 978-1-85411-508-9

A CIP record for this title is available from the British Library.

The publisher acknowledges the financial assistance of the Welsh Books Council.

Cover photo courtesy NASA earth observatory.

Printed in Bembo by Bell & Bain Ltd., Glasgow.

Author's website: www.hilarymenos.co.uk

Mixed Sources
Product group from well-managed
forests and other controlled sources
www.fsc.org Cert no. TT-COC-002769
© 1996 Forest Stewardship Council

FSC

Contents

Gift

I want to write you a small square poem
that starts with space and a vague notion of form
then pitches in headlong – not holding its nose
at the pull of another body – to atmosphere,
the curve of coastline, a fjord's fold and wrinkle,
borders, boundaries, the abrupt hyphenation of dams,
and hurtles through the sprawl of domes and spires
of a small Italian town to a piazza where,
between candy-stripe carts of ice-cream sellers,
past lunchtime chatter, waiters bringing *Lavazza*
and orange juice, it finds firm ground,
lands on the page like a flag, like a map of a world
impossible to resist and, catching the wind,
unfurls and soars like a bird circling the square.

Off My Trolley

Pushing my trolley today I have Ingomar the barbarian.
He is my shopping buddy. He strides through the fresh meat section
advising me on barbarian cuisine in the nineteenth century.
He is unimpressed by shrink-wrap and buy-one-get-one-free,
in fact the whole concept of payment is alien; shopping as raid.
I have learned that he likes his meat raw, grilled or fried,
but stews are for *stentl*, a dialect word which doesn't translate
but involves mice, your mother, and a failure to fornicate.

Fourteen years times fifty two weeks I have wrestled this trolley
trying to find a way to make incomes and outcomes tally.
Ingomar says compared to barbarism it's sheer fucking hell,
especially the queues, give him branding or besieging any day.
I find his outlook refreshing, but I know he won't stay.
Besides, next week I've got Elvis, the week after, Galway Kinnell.

Berg

After the Larsen breakout of ninety-five,
when a mound the size of Rutland calved with a howl
into the Admunsen sea, and bergy bits and growlers
surrounded Cape Longing, we were on standby.

Glaciologists from Colorado to London
argued over fracture mechanics and bed forms.
Every satellite map looked like a storm
breaking. We put a watch on the ice tongue.

Now everything mattered; melt water ponding,
the crystallography of frazil ice, the hole in the ozone layer,
the thermodynamics of polar-bear hair.
We sandbagged East Anglia, Holland.

They came like brides, majestic over Barking Reach,
queued to check-in at the Barrier, their tabular tops
reflecting weak sun, waltzed towards Wapping
and Wandsworth, cold and hooded, each one

like an inmate from some asylum holding the flowered
hem of her ancient slip too high up her pale thighs,
a thousand mile stare in her eyes,
saving the last dance for the Post Office Tower.

Cirque Tzigane

The Ringmaster speaks only Spanish and French.
He looks like The Cat in the Hat from Dr Seuss,
his nose tipped skywards, peering down at us
in the cheap seats. They are all cheap seats,

the tent has seen better days, as has the horse.
The Brittany Gazelle turns out to be a goat,
and who ever heard of performing cats? But he
has us all transfixed. He juggles a million balls,

nodding in time to the music when he faults
as if to say 'you see, that trick is just too hard
for even me'. Balancing on the trapeze,
he flexes and leaps. I'm holding my breath for him,

for the frayed rope. There's a moment of unease
when the horse gets a hard-on; a frisson of fear
when the nervous girl steps onto the rising stack
of planks and glass and teeters, and teeters, and holds.

Like Henry the goose coaxed onto his bed of nails,
we are spellbound by this man with dirty hands
and bright eyes making music we all seem to know
with nothing more than a cello bow and a saw.

Staverton Ghat

I squat in the shallows, rub bone-grey clay
over my baking skin. Dogs pant in the shade.
Bikes lie abandoned, tangled with Indian balsam
and common mallow. You are three years dead.

My children wade downstream. I can't forget
the job the Co-op did on you: your face
packed and painted. A boy floats past, belly up
like a dead calf, pale against shadow green.

Someone is lighting a fire, someone complains,
smoke shrouds the bank and out of the murk
an ancient song grows. In the confusion
I stoke up the fire and shoulder you on to the blaze.

Strange to watch a body sprawl and burn,
like meat, like wax, like lard. Dogs drool.
Kids throw pine cones into the flames.
The man who complained is shaking my hand

saying 'shantih, shantih, shantih'. We start to chant
as a tourist boat drifts by with crowds on deck
launching flotillas of candles on tin plates.
A ticker-tape blizzard of rose petals cascades.

From the tops of tall trees my children laugh
and call to me like birds, and when they fly,
the beat of their wings barely ruffling the air,
I see each silhouette bright against a burnt sky.

Geronimo

Button B eases the chair back and here I go
heels over head at the mercy of Linda, tidy in blue
scrubs and fetching mask-and-binocular combo.

I am agog for her latex probe, her precision drill.
Head bowed, anointed with Dettol, she bestows
her tender ministrations, and another gold filling,

one more macabre trophy for the kids, who joke
about prising them from my mouth after I die.
Consider the walk they must one day make

to the sea, perhaps, or some crumbling stone circle
to offer dust back to the earth in gritty scoops,
fingers scraping the box until they curl

blindly round a fused lump, like the collectible toy
gleaming at the bottom of the cereal packet,
an ivory plastic bust of Crazy Horse or Sitting Bull,

a two-inch model pyramid or erupting Popocatepetl
or Thunderbird Four in die-cast yellow metal.

Judgement

at Lang's Slaughterhouse, Ashburton

Lloyd is an angel, wings stuffed down the back
of disposable whites and strapped to his ribs
with the cord of his rubber bib. His cheeks are soft.
He has three knives and light starts from the blades.

Gordon is the angel of death. His apron is green.
We cross the disinfectant trough into the lairage.
"Hell's Kitchen" says Gordon. He checks passports.
The captive bolt sits lightly in his hands.

Lloyd hooks and hoists a beast. He slits its throat
and Prince's Purple Rain pours from the tannoy.
Danny angles his saw. His halo is blinding today.
The tattoos on his arms leap like blue flames.

Out the back, Gordon leans into a metal barrow
like a charity shopper, slices through stomach walls.
The tripe goes for dog food. The frilled bags hang
like small coats in a school cloakroom, stinking.

Down the line, the inspector stands by his rack of tongues
wearing a hairnet. And here's Tom, with his clipboard
and pen, his quiet smile. If you want blood,
there is blood. If you want men, here are men.

Siberian Sherbert

When orange snow fell and it wasn't a metaphor
for anything, even though it was Eastern Bloc,
the Moscow Met Office claimed it was red sand
whisked up by a Kazakhstani squall
and unloaded over the Omsk city walls, the soft peaks
of the Oblast hills, in a literal declaration of war.

The steppe looked like Frozen Mango Pudding.
The village of Pudinskoye had been Tangoed.
Novosti reported a glut of Siberian sherbert.
In the search for truth and justice, things got surreal.
We torched the forest, flames scorching the black dirt,
and drove our proud bears into the Taukum desert.

Extra Maths

My father is giving me extra maths. I am ten.
If one tap fills the bath at the rate of a litre a minute
and one fills the bath at the rate of a gallon an hour
and water escapes from the plughole at two pints a second
how long before we can take a bath?

I stand on one leg. My brother is watching TV.
Outside the other kids are bombing the hill on a go-kart.
My father gouges his pipe with his penknife,
dumping black tar into his cold baked beans.
My mother hates it.

Upstairs, water seeps over the rolled enamel rim,
steals down the side of the bath and through the boards,
easing its way down the white plastic flex
of the light fitting over my father's head
at a rate incalculable to man.

A Hundred Million Francs

He couldn't write it today. These days the kids
from the Rue des Petits-Pauvres have guns of their own.
Berthe and Mélie are working the Ponceau Road.
Gaby and Fernand run doorstep scams in Les Marches.
Philip Pullman's favourite – the inspiration for Lyra –
has a Perfect Pooch grooming parlour on the Rue Piot
and won't give so much as an inch of salon space
to the flea-ridden curs from the Fabourg-Bacchus farms.

Zidone and Juan are out of their heads on smack,
too old to care about carnival masks, spangles, castanets.
Sometimes they dream of multicoloured streamers
cascading to a floor awash with crêpe, and wake numb.
Today's factory is fully alarmed with CCTV and guards,
and the bangers – once twists of powder in bright paper,
now 'pyrotechnics' – are stored in child-proof boxes
away from a naked flame, and licensed for use.

As for the dogs, the toffs of the Quartier-Neuf
are tattooed and chipped and gendarmes appear like magic
the minute one crosses the Rue de la Vache Noire.
The mangy rabble of mongrels from the Bas-Louvigny
have long ago been shot for their taste in postmen.
Cité Ferrand has been cleansed, and Marion's own,
the stars of the story, Butor and Fanfan, have boils,
are blind, and haven't chased a real cat in years.

The Clos Pecqueuex has been earmarked for urban renewal
so the depots and *fabriques* will be knocked down
for designer flats a short drive along dog-free streets
to the malls of the Centre Ville – all rich pickings
for Pepé, Roublot and Ugly, who will never forget
the hot breath of a dog's maw, but are planning their next
heist, having run out of ready cash some time ago,
because a hundred million francs isn't worth what it was.

Road Runner

Give me a world where, when you fall in love
your heart leaps out of your chest
in the shape of a heart
and beats like a cuckoo sprung from its clock

where greed is announced by the ching!
of an opening cash box
and dollar signs roll on each eyeball,

where body parts stretch over miles and retain the shape
of whatever banged into them last,
frying pan, lamp post or garden rake,

and where, if you run off a cliff
you pause, suspended in air for one eternal second,
then fall a million miles onto rocks below,
with a cry that fades to a tiny puff of smoke

and next minute you're back.

Ark

Deep in the Arctic Circle, age-old drop-off for the Pole,
this is Svalbard, these blue fjords, these snowfields
studded with tracks of reindeer, arctic fox, and vole.

Near Longyearbyen, men stooped to carve a chamber
in the mountain's quiet heart. They planted seeds
beneath permafrost; slid off across its icy camber.

In four-ply foil pouches, sealed, air-locked, frozen,
a bank box full of blueprints, watched over by walrus,
patrolled by bears adrift on glacier mint ice floes.

Something there is that slips past stone and cement,
lifts steel from steel. Shoots test the air and the barren
mountain sprouts like a grotesque garden ornament,

a terracotta head with cress hair and wild alfalfa beard,
a grizzled green man, foliage tumbling like magma
to bag and carpet the land as the darkness recedes.

In The Night Garden

On Wednesday they raised the level of alert to five
on a scale of six. Lean hog and pork belly futures
took a dive in the Chicago trading pit and on Globex.
Smithfield marshalled its legal trouble-shooters.

Russia and China banned US pork imports.
Three hundred thousand pigs were slaughtered in Egypt.
In unfortunate scheduling at CBeebies headquarters
Igglepiggle had a massive fit of the sneezies.

With four-inch screamers stoking global alarm
and a crisis in factory food production at hand
we hitched up the box, drove to the back of beyond
and brought three Berkshire weaners on to the farm.

On Thursday I filled in movement forms,
scrawled standstill dates in chalk on the scullery wall,
tried not to think about all those tonnes of flesh
made meat in our name, and the trubliphone rang

shrill to the bedtime hour, and through my dreams
all the way to Friday's Lost Blanket episode,
where something was wrong. Upsy Daisy was in bed,
cold, her rainbow dreads slack, her Daisy Doo done.

Today the gilts are snouting daisies in the long grass.
Igglepiggle boards his little boat and waves good-night,
or is it good-bye, his thin mast tilting at the wind,
the anchor-light a pinprick in the furious dark.

gilt - young female pig

Cohiba

Along the Malécon, waves chivvy the cars,
old Studes and Chevys – all iconic wrecks.
Long stemmed palms hang ragged far off,
pinioned by wind. A man with no shoes asks me,
'Lady, where you from? You want cigar?'

In Partagas, on Industria, behind the Capitolio,
we crowd the factory floor, peering at hands
which, fifty times a day, wrap a slug of tobacco
in a lace-edged leaf and turn it, smooth and brown,
into something money can't buy in the USA.

Castro's favourite smoke was a Montecristo Grande,
cedar boxes keep the moisture in and, no,
they won't take Yankee dollars in the shop.
Noon sun beats the blinds down;
salsa pounds from precarious speaker stacks.

I want them to jump up onto their benches and sing,
using six-inch Churchills as mics, like there's no
tomorrow, like something from *Fame*. But it's just us,
me and the Irish girl and the French Canadians
wagging our hips like we knew how, in our dreams.

The Joy of Fitze

Numbers Forty-seven and Three mooch down the hill
haunch to haunch like a couple of loved-up dykes
lunchtime boozy in Seasalt and sensible shoes

each taking a turn to stand, a turn to mount. Three
lies her head flat along Forty-seven's back
and their huge eyes roll. I'm thinking Cold Comfort

as we slap and cajole them into the handling pen
where Roger Fitze waits with his hi-tech turkey baster,
a magnum of short straws on ice in his van.

Fitze has a Bajan tan. He's been in Texas
learning to PD cows at 32 days, the all American way.
He shakes his head, spills a swirl of liquid gas.

It's like a pip. He motions, and the calf's life
slips through his fingers, the fern-like curl of a backbone,
the perpetual dive of soft hooves.

To tell you the truth, he says, after thirty years
they can't teach me much. He strips off plastic gloves,
bundles them into wet grass. Nice to be home,

though the R&R in Barbados gets the thumbs up
even with hurricane Dean thrashing the island.
Bit blowy, says Fitze, with a wide mahogany grin

and I see him standing square, full face to the fray,
a bunch of palm tree trunks clasped in each hand
to anchor us all against the rum punch of the wind.

PD To test whether a cow is in calf (Pregnancy Determined)

One Trick Pony

Squirting cream conditioner into my palm,
I have to look to check that the tipped cap
has two holes, to explain the double spurt,

which flicks me back in time to that porn film
we watched one night, your hand up my skirt,
both pausing to wonder how the bloke on screen
had got the job – paunchy, bald, not well-hung –

then doing a double-take and, gob-smacked,
rewinding the tape to prove that what we'd seen
was a double stream like a forked tongue
licking the moan off the face of the honey.

You called him a one-trick pony, pushed me
down on the double bed, like you always did.
I knew then I had to quit this one-horse town.

Clan

those who make cups and bowls
the included ones
the lesser ruthless ones
those that are trained
those who mumble
collectors of dried dung
those with saddle sores
the not humans
those whose animals grow fat later than others
the cone-heads
those who are rich
those having red goats
those that belong to the Emperor
the embalmed ones
suckling pigs
mermaids
fabulous ones
stray dogs
those included in the present classification
those that tremble as if they were mad
innumerable ones
those drawn with a very fine camelhair brush
others
those that have just broken a flower vase
those that from a long way off look like flies

My Sometime Farmer

At night in my city-girl's bed
between crisp unwrinkled sheets
I dream my sometime farmer back from the dead.

His hands were rough as rope
and he snored like a squall. I barely slept
with him in my bed. He was up and away at dawn.

This was a man to love. He beat his life
like a forest fire, driving us all before.
I found the beauty in Beast, the beast in the man.
And the heat came off him like sulphur.

He lives out there in the fields, lives on the cliffs
where the wind whips foam from the breakers
and loads the air with salt. Keen as a knife,
he brought me to my senses, left me there.

Bernard Manning Plays Totnes Civic Hall

When Bernard Manning played Totnes Civic Hall
the whole town came along. Some bought tickets;
some came to picket in a constructive and caring way.
Terence sang a protest song. We thanked him for sharing.

The wiccans wore woad. Ash sold poems on parchment.
Sky from Tantric Turkeys burned calming patchouli,
assertively chanting the mantra "battery farming
fucks with your karma, man". Bootiful, said Bernard.

The staff of Dartington College took front row seats
in an act of guerrilla theatre. Post-modern, ironic,
Bernard didn't know and didn't care; to him they were
just punters, paying full fare, and not in wheelchairs.

He opened with a sure-fire joke about a gay agoraphobic
who came out and went straight back in, provoking
most of the punters at once, especially the womyn
from Diptford Dykes for Psycho-social Wellbeing.

His carefully chosen gags about wellies and sheep
went down like a fat lamb in slurry. The Mayor had a fit
at his mother-in-law routine. High on quinoa and ginseng,
even the hippies joined in as the crowd stormed the stage.

Bernard fled. As his Roller sped off up the High Street
and shrank to the size of a lentil, the townsfolk united
in transcendental glee. Someone (it may have been me)
said, "That's five hundred quid well spent".

Face of America

They had to sew her into the dress it was that tight,
tighter than a mermaid's skin and shimmered like scales.
Mother of God! You could see it in their eyes –
a hunger for what she'd got. Nobody knows
how she did it, but she looked for all the world
like someone who'd got all the answers. The big 'Yes'.

Every now and then beauty steps forward.
On a shell, a chariot, a podium. Rolled up in a rug.
And for one brief moment time itself steps back.
Then there's the fall, the war, the telephone call,
the men in suits with white powder, dusting for prints
and, up on a billboard, the face of America, smiling.

Tiramisu

Partially reconstituted Dried Skimmed Milk,
Glucose Syrup, Sugar, Water, Vegetable Fat,
Sponge [Wheat Flour, Sugar, Egg, Glucose Syrup,
Vegetable Fat, Raising Agents (E503, E450),
Potato Flour, Emulsifier (E471), Milk Proteins, Salt,

Flavouring], Marscapone Cheese (5%),
Alcohol, Marsala Wine (2.5%), Egg Yolk,
Fat Reduced Cocoa Powder, Stabilisers (Agar,
Xanthan Gum, E407), Dextrose, Coffee Extract,
Wheat Starch, Flavourings, Emulsifier (E471), Salt.

Fall

This is the sweet season. Black and red gums
decorate the hedge. Virginia creeper
every colour of peardrop swathes the shed,
and acorns range from cocoa to lime green.

I am pricking sloes for gin. Last year's crop
glows garnet on the shelf. A comb of honey
warms on the stove, luring drunken wasps.
Summers condense to this, and clothes outgrown.

On the floor, a Matchbox car, paint
peeling to lead grey. September steers us
towards Hallowe'en, relentless Catherine wheels,
bitter cordite and evenings dark early.

Around the eaves the martins dance aerobics.
The future goes all ways, like pick-up sticks.

Star Dust

Let's hear it for you alone one night, with your radio
tuned to a little light tango – Ramon Raquello,
live from the Park Plaza in downtown New York,
playing *Star Dust* – as breaking news transformed
a cattle shed in the lush New Jersey farmlands
into a beachhead for a war that was no war.

What did you think? – toe-tapping while the band
played *Verano Porteño* or listening to some
ventriloquist's dummy then turning the dial to find
Martians wading the wide Hudson River,
gorgons on stilts, their silver machines spewing
Greek fire, and the end of the world nigh.

Like lobbing a meteor into Grover's Mill pond
and watching the ripples reach. Henry Sears,
thirteen, avoiding homework, took the radio downstairs
to his mother serving beer from her tavern bar
and (this is part of the myth) a dozen men
jumped to their guns, shot down a water tower.

The radio withdraws into the night, and millions
traipse home, extras to another man's drama
which became their own. And what do we hold now,
which soon enough will burst in our fumbling hands?
Mars is a red disc swimming in a blue sea.
Fake is as old as the Eden Tree.

Minted

Wrestling with surgical snips and pale gristle
you cut the cord and declare this baby
open, like a summer fête, a launched ship.

I am queen of the bower, a green woman
lying in state, jeweled leaves snaking my cheeks,
crowned with wild mint and bay laurel.

Morning sun powers in, kicking our tea-lights
into touch. I bite down hard, testing the coinage
and the room yields slightly, stays bright and true.

Sleeping Lions

What did they tell her, that it was her
birthday, as they wound her round
that it was a fancy dress party
and she was a beautiful present for herself
a cake, a firework, a sky ray lolly?

Did they stroke her pretty hair
her rapt, round face? What did they say
as they chauffeured her through the winding streets
a special girl on her special day
in her best *abaya*?

Did they make it a game?
Pass the parcel. Musical bumps. Sleeping lions.
When the music stopped did she expect
a room full of banners and party poppers
where all her friends would jump out and shout "Surprise!"

*BAGHDAD Feb 1 2008 (ABC News) Down Syndrome Women
Used as Suicide Bombers*

Fantastic Voyage

Let me know when we pass the soul, he said,
which, in 1966, should have tipped us off
that he was the saboteur, the godless one. That
and his Nixon-like tendency to sweat.

The science was shaky, at best. But we were stuck
inside this psychedelic space-age set
in thrall to dubious special effects
and Raquel Welch's perfect swimsuit breasts.

We steered by pilotage – heart, lungs, arteries –
fuelled by a single nuclear particle
smug in its lead-lined box. Until it started to fail,
and the groovy lava-lights dimmed.

Without sun or stars, we fell back on tried and true
dead reckoning, reduced to slinging guns, tools,
anything that would drift, out of the craft
to see how long it took to pass the aft fin

like some throwback band of medieval sailors
mumbling chants passed down from father to son,
paying out cables of knotted hemp, counting fathoms,
watching flotsam slide past the rail.

We were way off course, desperate for a fix
when the doctor, peering into a purple haze,
saw the end of the optic nerve. We made our escape;
somehow always knew it would end in tears.

Honk!

Ici le Périgord, beloved of Englishmen
and geese, if the postcards are to be believed.
Here they are, plump and easy, strolling through fields
past ancient Périgourdin stone-built huts
with conical roofs. Geese with broad smiles.
Geese batting eyelashes, gingham cloths slung
loosely round suspiciously slender necks.

Each self-respecting supermarché in the region
has pyramids of tins stacked ceiling-high,
yellow fat streaming down like lazy champagne.
There's foie gras on every menu. Roadside signs
advertise it à vendre. And everywhere, and nowhere,
bloody geese. Bronze geese, geese as statuary,
silent and proud on a plinth in the Centre Ville.

Cluedo

He has mapped our future in black ink
on three sheets of paper. He unfolds them,
spreads them on the table in the pub,
smoothing them with hands that draw
a perfect circle, perfect straight line.

Our house rises to greet us, north elevation,
then hunkers down among the bunched contours
of the land survey. He plots parking,
a gravel drive, a porch to shelter friends
as they wait, clutching chardonnay, flowers.

The plans are detailed minutely, each stone
hand drawn. So clear I can almost see myself
dust. You in the study with the lead pipe,
me in the kitchen making jam, our perfect kids
playing, picking apples, riding bikes.

Contact

After you left I slunk upstairs like a lover
and saw, on the bedside table, next to the bed,
your lenses, neatly placed, one on top of the other
like glass bowls, stacked and gleaming, blurred
by your thumbprints and last night's whisky.
I thought about DNA and vanity and proof,
how we slept, your hand circling my wrist,
this strange, widespread exchange of half-truth,
delusion and private bargains hard struck.
Still not sure if I should chase after you, or why,
I paused for one crucial minute to take stock,
saw they were disposable and chucked them away.

Mass Rapid Transit

They rounded up the trannies down on Bugis Street,
showed them how a real truncheon feels.
Now Sugar plays nice in a doorway on Desker Road.
One for the guys back home, says Sport,
in ten dollar Chinese silk.

A round-the-island trip on the MRT
skims concrete jungle, ghosts of British troops
still wading through the coconut estates
en route to Chang's, singing as they march:
there'll always be an England.

Hawkers with hobs and neon signs
squat by makeshift stalls in the vast arcades
serving *laksa* and *tom yam plaa*
just feet from haute couture. Five hundred three-star
Happy Toilets™ flush when you stand up.

Round the clock the hooverboats suck scum
from the city's clogged artery
which laps the warehouses along Boat Quay.
In The Bomb Xplosive Entertainment Zone
we sink frozen margaritas over guidebooks that don't say

snakes are still found in urban Singapore –
the pit viper, the black spitting cobra –
coiled on low branches in the mangroves,
snug in a garbage bin in Fernhill Road,
rustling under your bed.

Floorboards

Floorboards, she said, with that typically French shrug
straight from Napoleon via Charles de Gaulle.
So all that summer we tiptoed round the flat
knowing Cecile was down there, being quiet.

Stairs were the worst, and August. We pissed in bowls,
refused to take the three steps down to the loo.
We slept on the living room floor, watched silent films,
ate cornflakes and cheap jam, whispered

about boundaries, how to manage the space
between people – that line of my father's – how
my right to swing my arm stops at your nose.
And underneath each stifled creak, Cecile.

We bought the screws, borrowed a friend's drill
but it was always too hot, or too early, or too late.
The ants were swarming. Sometimes Cecile played music,
its muffled drumbeat nudging our consciences.

Until we saw her load the van – eiderdowns,
a kettle trailing its flex – and watched her drive away.
We pulled the carpets up that night, screwed
down the boards. Days later, you went, too.

Neighbours

Stonechats chip and bounce above the hedge,
and swifts surf the breeze, their forked tails
flicking the vees, but this is not what we're here for.
Here comes Bob with his dogs. One barks, one bites.

John has the farm in the valley, peppercorn rent
but he's broke. Down a potholed track, old man Tucker
hawks and spits at crows. His bungalow lurks
by the barn. Sunset flushes the slurry gold.

When the wind is right we hear Nick shooting rats
and Kate screaming Stop, then just screaming.
She won't last long. There's a witch at Sparkwell Cross
– we keep our kids inside on ancient days.

Through the blue haze specked with long-leg flies I see Bob
tying baler twine round the neck of the one that barks.

Pub Quiz

In the Sea View Hotel, Arman pulls me a pint
of the local brew. It foams with salt.
It is pub quiz night and all the tables are laid.

Outside, salt plains glitter in the sun.
Trawlers cast long shadows on the bleached sea bed.
A sandstorm builds in the west.

Arman brings me a menu, but everything's off.
He tells me his dream, how the sea shrank.
Ten thousand Uzbek fishermen dredged a canal

but the fish died. Summers are too hot now,
and winters cold, and tourists don't come.
He keeps quiz night alive for the sake of the guests

though there are none, and there's only one question
written in red on his sheet. Dust settles
on the lethal tablecloths. I guess at the Aral Sea

but Arman says there are no winners here
and he can't help the chemical tang.
It is closing time. He bolts the window tight.

Honesty Box

We crossed on the ferry, a shivering boy on each lap
and the rucksacks between us. Salt scoured our cheeks.
Polruan was lifeless even at peak season,
the harbour wall easing up out of choppy water,

twenty slippery steps each fringed with weed.
We walked past shops selling faded souvenirs
with signs blistered by years of buffeting wind,
hauled the kids up the hill and the view grew with us,

Fowey stretched out along the other bank,
the black and yellow tugs, weak sun glancing
off the rails and, right up the estuary's throat,
English China Clay and the big gates.

At the top I watched you gazing out to sea, past
garages and ugly fifties flats. The boys crouched
in the shelter chalking on the bench, while a small
boat tacked against the tide, trying for home.

Back on the quay there were tulips for sale in a crate,
their sappy stems bundled in rubber bands.
"They'll wilt in the car," you said, and walked away.
I took a bunch and looked for the honesty box.

Meet Dave

Meet Dave, my builder. Six foot four, eyes blue,
hands loose at his sides. Remembers a time
when, starting out, his wife cooked hearts for tea.

Meet Dave, my sparks. Drills concrete blocks like lard,
bowls his spool of cable across the cobbled floor
like a tailor's cotton bobbin, like a girl's hoop.

Meet Dave, my lighting man. He drives a silver Mini,
checks lumen counts for fun, loves symmetry.
The other men grin at his neat hair, his neat shoes.

In the sitting room of my new cottage the Daves
discuss halogen spots, transformers and GU10s,
three different ways of shedding light on space.

They blink back dust from an angle grinder outside.
Dave's lighting scheme doesn't fit Dave's beams
but Dave the sparks thinks he knows how to sort it.

So unlike last time with you and the big house: lawsuits,
blame, the money gone. I wipe dust from my eyes,
say: "Back to the drawing board, Dave." All three turn.

Shake-out

The future is likely to see... a small but significant shake-out
of older farmers, few of which have a successor.
(Changes in the Structure of Agricultural Business – DEFRA)

Back along, 'shake-out' was what she did
to the day's clothes, turning them inside-out
with a snap that sent flurries of chopped hay
into the cobbled yard, teasing straw from seams
for fear of clogging the precious washing machine
(still new-fangled after nearly fifteen years).

Stiff from a day spent hoeing swedes by hand,
or shoring-up a mangel cave, he'd come home
to find the passage thick with the sweet-sour cloy
of raw milk priming the worn slate floor
and, in the farmhouse kitchen, the soft slap-
slap of butter forming slowly in the churn.

Up-country, in some air-conditioned room,
the suits report. His gaunt face stares them down
in black and white. 'Lowland. Pastoral. Remote.'
And now he drives a van. She sits at home.
The parlour is empty, swept and disinfected.
A dog with nothing to do patrols the yard.

Faithless

I knew him by his hair, more Gabriel
than Gabriel himself. And how sparks flew.
We went to it like wayward souls, him
shoved against the wall, shirt off,
poised for flight, knowing, like a sepia-tint
street-girl, debauched and glowing. I traced
the scalloped scars that straddled his spine.
Faithless. I made him mine.

At once the excuses: the distance, the cost.
When he said he was leaving I knew this a lesson
I'd already learnt. Once bitten, twice burnt.
Both blessed and cursed. Both lost.
Now nights are loose and strange. I deal in never,
but dream of an angel's rub and rush of feathers.

Hard Hat

I am still in the picture because, on that day,
I am wearing a brown and green jerkin,
three wide stripes, brown green brown,
which echo the broad bands of red and white
on the pipes of the processing plant. I stand
by a sign that says 'Hazardous Area,' trying to smile
while my father composes the shot.

There's a man in a suit standing near me
with a look on his face that says he doesn't know
how to react to the fact that his UK supplier
of hazardous area safety instrumentation
has brought his thirteen-year-old daughter along.
I come to know that look. I don't know the date.
I don't know the country. I had to wear a hard hat.

Buffalo State Lunatic Asylum

It's a far cry from the furious bedlam of Barnum and Bailey's
Greatest Show on Earth, the carnival peddlers, the circus parade,
the Big Top with its three rings and curious human menagerie:
Chang and Eng, Tom Thumb, the Fiji mermaid in its glass case,

and us, the seven singing Sutherland sisters, each with our hair
brushing the floor, end to end the tresses measuring thirty-seven feet,
Fletcher working the crowd with our patent Hair Grower, Restorer,
Scalp Cleaner, Combs, his life as a preacher clearly not yet over.

The weight of my hair made me mad. I was locked in my room
then in this chill place with its long corridors, its iron beds.
Like an ancient Rapunzel, my dress growing tight round my middle,
I sit at the window grille and sing, still combing my heavy hair.

Men in Cars

They park up, on the verge, sprawl in their seats,
spread newspaper over their laps, Kleenex to hand,
briefcases lolling agape on the leather beside them.

Do they have homes, wives, jobs, or do they
inhabit a wholly tarmac-ed world where the only
things that register are pile-ups, road-works, rain

and undertaking the jerk in the outside lane;
do they cruise the hard shoulder, burn rubber for fun,
circle the M25, plan day trips out to Preston,

Truro, Hull, pore over Ordnance Survey maps
in search of a B road they've never driven before,
somewhere deep in the rural rump of Wiltshire

two miles from a pub with a decent pint where the sun
bursts through the canopy of leaves to dapple the road
and they can pull onto the grassy edge by a bank

brimming with maidenhair, milkwort, redshank,
cuckoo spit daubing a froth of Baby Blue Eyes,
a riot of foxgloves thrusting out of the mound,

a heady smorgasboard of shaft and stem
that explodes in their face as they wind the window down
and wait for the ticking as the engine cools to a stop.

Mistress

Polish Anna writes: "Please let me know
where you laid him to rest, finally."
She wants to pay her respects to a handful of ash
buried under the spread of the apple tree
in the garden of the house where I was born,

in a hole barely a spade's width, spade's depth,
and me concerned about speeches, and dogs,
then picking flowers and balancing them
on a mound that looks less like a burial site
and more like a small repair in Astroturf.

I carry his empty box back in, jangling
four screws in my pocket, knowing the house
will be sold, and he with it, still not sure
if that was the best place for him, wondering what
you and all the others would have done.

So I put off writing back to you, in your tiny
Warsaw flat, partly to preserve the equilibrium
of new owners, Mr and Mrs Patel, but more,
because I do not really know where
or indeed if I have laid him to rest, finally.

Linus

The drugs go in through a tube up his nose,
come out again as multicoloured vomit –
phenytoin pink, red iron and the vitamins'
gold stain – a curdled rainbow on the babygro.
He makes a guessing game of dosages.
Horizons shrink to a silver line. Remember him,
small on a small bed, wrapped in foil for warmth,
like a turkey, too early for Christmas.

They sent me to a basement lined with lead,
squat grey breast-pumps stationed round the room
like ancient sewing machines. Hydraulics hissed
as they milked me numb. I woke curled round him,
screened by curtains, pillows laid on the floor,
crisp white squares to break his fall.

Man of Steel

Superman is alive and well and living in South Brent.
I saw him this morning pushing a buggy with one hand,
pulling a stubborn toddler with the other, child and father
conjoined in a strange *pas de deux* in a stranger ballet.

He orders tea and an iced bun in Crumbs 'n' a Cuppa,
fills in the resistration for his hour on the fourth plinth.
He's crucified by the bastard CSA, broke by Tuesday.
The money, at least, goes faster than a speeding bullet.

Some days he has to rip open his shirt to check he's still
himself, that red and yellow shield, the curled 'S'.
No-one wants a hero so he's traded steel for satire,
subversion, and the slow collapse of his muscled belly.

These days he feels like the only man on planet Earth,
the only boy with a dad like Marlon Brando.
He crouches behind a cold chimney on a cold rooftop,
x-ray vision eyes burning with self-belief,

wraps his plastic cape of angel's wings around him,
planning a retcon, a re-boot, the comeback of all time,
and the Devon skies above him pulse with promise.
He does it all for Dean, aged four, and baby Billy.

Gathering Dust

Today I am gathering dust,
watching motes in a shaft of light
weave a double-helix to the sun,
thinking of those I have lost, losing the thread.

Small things come to mind.
Their particular motion describes
boots on a bridge, a bottle, wayward tracks,
an infinite number of ways up, or down.

Temptation is to slip sideways
through that shimmering migrainous line
into one of the countless other worlds
that shift, diverge, spin off in fracted code

coming back to the place where we first
found true chanterelles nosing their yellow frills
through layers of autumn leaves,
back to a time before it was too late.

One for Sorrow

Do they lurk in the branches waiting for us to pass
so that one smug individual can casually fly out
while the rest titter into their feathers, smirking, "Sorrow!"

I think they should be forced to bond for life,
literally. A rolling programme, nationwide, using
small metal bands. Cheap at twice the price.
The Chancellor could fund it under Mental Health Care.

Then they too would hobble and flap, each pulling
a different way, pecking and fighting but having to declare
to all who passed, in a strained shriek, "Joy!"

Ephemeroptera

Will we look back on this, this day of days
where we partied and paired, shone and danced, made deals

the like of which were never done before,
then swarmed with angels to shed our rude concerns

like snowfall in cold light? If we can speak, then,
what should we defend? We are all dishonoured by the past.

And what do you say, you who would, without thought,
have fisted the world into a small green ball

and stuck it in your mucky pocket for keeps?
How will you plead, on the day?

Douce Ambience

The cow in the slurry pit is booming, making a sound
like the Partridge Island foghorn, warning all hands
of rocks, shoals, headlands, and such dangers to shipping
as are generally found in a farmyard. House martins
bombard the shippen roof, backlit by the May milk moon.

The boy let the bull out so we were all on edge,
four men not minding the gap in Mick's block-work
as the cow made a jink past the tractor, and plunged in.
There was a lot of bother with ropes and a heavy chain
but as night fell she was still stuck. There's always one.

Roger arrived with his shotgun and soft mouthed dogs.
I was all for high-tailing it over the fields but the cow
had other ideas and as she segued from Minor Swing
to Tears we were persuaded of the efficacy of jazz.
In these situations it pays to think out of the box.

So, she's more than three-quarters buried, swaybacked,
nose just clear of the crust, but she croons such a sweet
and lovely harmony to Douce Ambience, the chain slung
casually round her neck, the moon so low and large
I swear she could reach up and lick its cheesecake face.

Like the band on the Titanic, we count in another tune,
hoping she hasn't yet gone down. Look, she is using
optical Morse code, the age-old language of female cows
in shit, batting her pretty lashes and rolling her eyes.
Di-di-di-dah-dah-dah-di-di-dit. The song will be over soon.

Spin

I floored the gas. Wanted to see
what the old lady would do tanked up on super.
Forty fags on the dash and a quarter of scotch
snug in the glove. A warm bag of doughnuts.
Damp streaks on the leather.

It was one of those days
when every tune the radio plays is a classic.
Heat thrums off the tarmac. Everywhere you look
you see fashion shoots, record covers, Bacardi
ads in the making. Immortal days, pitched high.

I gunned the engine,
took the corner wide and, squinting,
spun into the noonday sun.

Pastoral

This was a hard calving, the one vet, matter-of-fact,
her arm sunk six joints deep in the flank of the cow,
the other buttressing the haunch, their sporadic chat
about the new 'green' Ford Focus, and the Practice lunch.

There was not much blood, though layers of flesh cut.
As we lugged the slack bundle from under her bones
it was all about keeping the cow upright where she stood
(a rope round her far hoof, both of us ready to haul)

and the slight smell of steak, and when the calf finally
shuddered a breath we draped him across a straw bale.
Then one got to sewing, the other to stopping the rumen,
the bagged uterus, all of it, tumbling into the mud.

When she was done with the needle and nylon thread
she strode to the calf, still caught in his own thick phlegm,
and in one smooth move slung him over the gate to drain,
his curled coat slippery, his lovely head hung low,

froth streaming into the grass, and he bucked at her slap
and the cow at last made her long drawn out soft moo
to call and claim him, while the hills all around spun slower
with us at the hub, by the gate, in this makeshift pen.

Personal Ad

Your poems are like the personal ads
in the London Review of Books

*Scarlet-sabled Seburg, lost in translation Tottenham Court Road Tube,
it's true: we can't say sayonara – only adieu. Box no. 07/21*

I quote verbatim,
though you would dispute 'verbatim'

*Intrepid alpha M public finance lecturer, 54, WLTM Antipodean Axa
with a view to treehouse blitzkrieg. Box no. 05/16*

at first I think they mean well
and are clearly trying to do something

*I'm a fish but you're a dish. Part ichthyic, part batrachian M seeks
another turn in the jacuzzi with the Aqua Marina of N16.
Box no. 06/12*

but I do not understand
what you want to say

*Andromeda-fixated thirty-something poof.
Damn sure I'm not the only one in here. Box no. 05/03*

and am left with a vague sense
that you are simply being clever

The colostomy bag is an Alessi at box no. 06/11

which unfortunately for you
doesn't do it for me

My ideal woman is a man. Sorry, mother. Box no. 04/08

so I have decided to write
a poem that suits us both

Box no. 02/14. As if you could even afford an Aga. Peasant.
Box no. 06/08

plain speaking poet, F, 39, WLTM
emperor, clothed. Box no. 05/09

Reunion

Thirteenth century portraits frown from the panelled walls.
The seating plan puts me with Tom who I fondly recall
as the college drunk. Our children share a consultant.
We talk kidneys over the starter, divorce through the beef.

All through the speeches my mind is half on the Queen's toast
and half on watching a man who I slept with once
deal to his pin-striped neighbour. I make for the bar
where someone is smoking Havanas and quoting Proust

and I'm lectured on insider dealing, patents and third world debt
till I find myself thinking of you in the big shed,
easing life into a cold world, overalls torn,
hands purple with iodine, stinking of chain oil and sheep shit.

Moulin du Chaos

Huelgoat, Brittany

The guide promised menhirs to test Obelix,
a carpet of ochre leaves, a canopy of gold,
and a fix of crêpes. We were sold a pretty story.
Nobody told us about this bawdy tumble,
these splayed knees, these lewd and lolling thighs,
a geologist's wet dream in all its glory.

No total support affair in beige Spandex and wire,
no whalebone corsetry or fine steel bands
could hold these basalt fists. Like beached seals,
swollen and mottled with cold, they formed
an igneous centrefold, bumping and grinding
all the way down the valley's little v.

And when we came to the Roche Tremblante
no shove, no tender touch, could trigger its shudder
and all we could do was shrug and walk away,
retrace our steps to the pont and hold each other
while water under our feet battered the sluice,
plunging off in torrents lathered with grey.

Slaughterhouse

Let it be done here, here where death
is all in a day's work, and by men who deal
in the thing itself. Spare me a slow decline,
years of pain and pills, months in bed,
weeks of too few visits, then too many.

Instead, give me a brief and rollicking ride
through Devon lanes, sun striating my face,
a gentle nudge out of the truck and into the gates
of the cattle race, the open arms of the crush
and the captive bolt's blind kiss.

Roll me over the grid in the next room
into the warm and expert hands of these,
the last men on earth to hold me; men skilled
in the precise and subtle use of knives,
the exercise of necessary force.

Then winch me through to where the others hang,
trimmed and tagged, bumping haunch to haunch,
couched in the companionable chill.

Matriochka

Deep in the hills outside Moscow
in the model village crawling with men in tights
was a stall selling *matriochka*, nesting dolls,
l'une dans l'autre – like mother like daughter –
painted headscarves slick to their Slavic cheeks,
the smallest of every trio a stumped baby,
featureless, red gloss, arms at its sides.

Each night I come to the bar of the Hotel Mir,
its rampant Soviet Classicism wrenching my guts,
and watch in dazed slow motion the jug
crash to the floor, the jostling cubes pent up,
released, to skitter across parquet between legs
and all heads turn, the dolls twisting at the hip,
their babies jolting inside them.

Sundowner

We were drinking Icebreakers and Jungle Joes
at Nero's in the meatpacking district, not knowing
this was the end of an era. News came in

that Boudicca, the British bitch, was dead,
wedged in a gorge somewhere on Watling Street,
her lines of retreat blocked by her own wagons,

her barbarian troops barrel-shot, her bright mane
ground in the mud. Claret on the cobbles. Canapés
and a tray of Kabul Coolers on the house.

Nero ordered the goatfish special to celebrate,
and a pitcher of Vertigo, pledging to paint
the whole of New York City Forth Bridge Red.

The bloody thing was alive. That was a shock.
It hung at the table, its blotched flanks livid,
its goatee barbels waving in slow rebuke,

drowning in a sauce of its own liver.
We watched it fade from vermillion to bruise blue
to a rosy shimmer, ate it poached with a wine jus

then rinsed it down with a double Double Vision.
The highs just kept on coming. Till I saw the TV,
flames in someone's eyes, and looked outside

to a city on fire, and Nero loving it karaoke-style,
serenading his own phizog, his gurning mug
plastered on the front of tomorrows dailies.

I knew the show would end with a White Lady.
I downed it, got my coat, left my tab unpaid,
felt her ice-cold hands meet around my throat.

Wish

When you look up at me with those great
blue eyes so like my own, and get busy
on the breast, whatever stuff it is kicks in
surprising me with a plain kind of peace

and I, who still feel like Henny Penny
forever ducking the sky and blind to the fox
wish you only safe passage on this earth
and more than enough love to live by.

Acknowledgements

Acknowledgements are due to the editors of the following journals where some of these poems first appeared: *Envoi, Magma, Mslexia, nth-position, Orbis, Smith's Knoll, Staple, The Independent on Sunday, The North, The Wolf.*

Prizes:

'Pastoral' won second prize in the *Mslexia* Poetry Competiton, 2009.

'Moulin du Chaos' was commended in the Buxton Poetry Competition, 2009.

'Sundowner' was a runner-up in the *Mslexia* Poetry Competition, 2008.

'The Joy of Fitze' won a supplementary prize in the Bridport Poetry Competition, 2008.

'Berg' was a runner-up in the BBC Wildlife Magazine Poet of the Year Competition, 2006.

'Off My Trolley' was a runner up in the *Mslexia* Poetry Competition, 2006.

'Bernard Manning Plays Totnes Civic Hall' was highly commended in the Peterloo Poetry Prize, 2006.

'Face of America' won first prize in the *Envoi* Poetry Prize 2003.

Some of the poems were published in the pamphlet *Extra Maths* (Smith/Doorstop Books, 2004) and some were published in the *Oxford Poets 2007* anthology (Carcanet, 2007).

Thanks to my family and friends, especially my husband Andy Brodie, my sons Jethro, Bruno, Linus and Inigo, and my mum Janet. Thanks also to Candy Neubert, Julie-ann Rowell and Christopher Southgate for advice and support, and to Barbara Bridger for the first push.